DANDELIONS & OTHER FLOWERS
©2014 Daniel J. Cox

ISBN: 978-1495315091

Book and cover design: Michael Campbell, MC Writing Services
Cover art: Daniel J. Cox

DANDELIONS
& OTHER FLOWERS

DANIEL J. COX

For Nancy –

because there should have been
so much more than flowers etched in stone
and a wolf howling in the night

Contents

Foreword

I always wanted to be a writer (when I didn't want to be a cowboy…or a cowboy writer). I graduated from Tarkio College at the end of 1972 with a degree in English, but there were no jobs. I couldn't even get into one of the Armed Services. My father encouraged me to go back and get my teaching certificate ("Teachers can always get jobs!") and continue to write. I taught for seven years before it finally came to me that I had always been teaching. My writing, however, became an occasional poem or letter to the editor of the local newspaper. He urged me to keep at it, as did my mother and my wife. Lesson plans and student essays just took up too much writing time and energy. Now I have lots of time to observe and think and write. So I've been writing. Unfortunately, those three people who supported me for so long are all gone. Every line in this book I owe to them. I hope they know how grateful I am and always have been.

Living City

Black and blue housefly wanders purposefully in,
Out among the tomato soup cans, soured, crusted
Milk cartons, rusted springs of unstuffed sofas;
His song nauseates the putrid air.

Catbird sings to his yellow-striped namesake prowling,
Padding, knocking over lamp shades shading the eyes
Of the near-sighted rat chewing crinkly-nose on the
Green Giant's corn.

Blacksnake slides easily, crushingly around the beetle-eaten
Corpse of the once-thirsty mongrel rotting in the heavy
Sun of an acidic afternoon.

Honey-bee passes by, passes by the staggering,
Limping, long forgotten Forget-Me-Not dripping life on
So much dead around it.

Clouds open their sleepy mouths and yawn their salty tears.
Saturday's bath finds a Sunday mannequin crisp and
Shining in its polished nakedness. Tree frog
Spits between its toes on the back of a plastic neck.

Someone throws another sackful on the heaping stench.
Hungry eyes rush to find tomorrow's feast.

1/24/1971

Roast Pork

Lying there
Steaming in spiced deliciousness, your
Olive eyes squealing in mute surprise,
How ridiculous you look,
Gumming your favorite fruit.

You tried all your short life to
Get to those ripe berries before they fell
From the tree. Now you don't even
Know that it's been placed within easy reach

Even if you did
It wouldn't do any good.
You're too dead to close your mouth.

2/7/1971

To Kiss a Stranger

(On Matthew 27:3-10)

Sparkling, shining seduction
Spilling through holy
Stained fingers.

Cruel covenant, forsaken twice,
Buys an end for strangers
And for kings.

Born for betrayal,
Both hang from
Separate trees.

2/22/1971

Twice Lost

half-
way.

half-way there
    and
back.

You could have made it all the way...

same distance.

3/17/1971

21 March

blue-black wings
churning
late March winds
raise
harping mists of curiosity
over
half-awakened
birth.

3/18/1971

Burnt Fingers

white-hot intensity
ignites
leaving one
fullness
rushing high-crest to
burst
Fourth-of-July-rocket
colored
in my eyes with
Pain.

3/18/1971

Midnight Cowboy

Four black hats
firing
thirtysixshotswithoutreloading
expire traditionally
as John Wayne
kisses
his girl
goodbye.

3/29/1971

As on a Darkling Plain

A hidden moon with silver hands
    casts shadows on the mist.
Trees, like silent spectres, haunt
    grey waves of moving grass.

Melting into frozen dreams,
    forgotten sleepless nights make
Instant, running colors fade
    to ghosts in mute parade.

5/8/1971

Almost By

with my head turning
forgetting circles
quiet, drifting pictures
I have tried to put away
shout misty agonies at me

one more
I won't remember
two
your face studies with me
silence
long moments touching
fingertips
faraway lips

gone
remembered
floating by
wanting nothing –
the day before
no pain

roads stretch before me
going all directions
by your window
where I don't want to be

forever is a lonely word
forgetting is forever
almost

1/12/1972

Missouri Calling

Cities crowd me too much:
>bumper-to-bumper engine noises and flashing lights
>sit on my mind and body and make it hard to
>see and hear and breathe 'til I can only live
>dreams and weekends.

I am coming to the hills of freedom, the running streams
>of life and laughter.

There, beneath the clouds still white, swimming in
>the songs of alive and clean birds, alongside the
>startled grunting of deer and heart-stopping
>whir of frightened quail...

I will be one of those people bare-footed and tapping
>and listening to Missouri calling –

Fiddle-strings and catfish whiskers and long, hickory smoke
>days.

7/17/1975

Home Again

Too many summers and winters, springs and falls
    keep me away from the flour,
    and Band-Aids, proud smiles, and reproaches
    when my heart calls.
I can't just cry and know that any hour
    there'll be the warm arms, companion tears,
    and always the knowing "It'll be alright; you can do it"
    to ease my terrible doubts and fears.
The many falls and summers, springs and winters
    have taught me that I can and will
    make the best of my life because of hers,
    but there are the days and nights
    I need her still.
When I can go no more on my own strength
    and the arms I want to lean on can be no other's,
    I run away to my memories and, at length,
    find the peace and the hope I always received
    from my mother.

10/12/1978

American Phoenix

We stood and watched our brave young eagles dare
to see how high, how fast, how far they might
wing outward to the limits of the air
and then beyond, into the starry night.

With courage and with joy each one flew on,
a challenger of the unknown and all
of those who fear and cry that we have gone
too far and now, with wings aflame, must fall.

And with the triumphs that we all would share
will come the ashes of the times we fail.
But to succeed then we must greatly dare,
for in new victories our losses pale.

This eagle, like the phoenix, folds its wings,
then from the fires bursts forth and soars and sings.

1/28/1986

The Exchange

I	do
believe that we can	take this day and
make of our communion	Tomorrow as promised
by the love we share	a lifetime of becoming
one vision, one hope,	one in love and understanding
that you and I will always be	the little moments that
we	do... .

1/26/1980;
rev. 6/03/2004

Portrait of the Artist as Teacher

(or the Teacher as Artist)

Da Vinci stands
between a wheel and canvas
unfinished, musing
      while I
      in van Rijn shadow
      flecked with old clay, fumble with a brush
      (the details of my life lie dark around me –
      background, perspective, inspiration, sanctuary –
      yet in this light, new vision clarifies old dreams)
      and realize
      I cannot be
      the final fire or frame.
      Yet already I have
      turned the wheel
      mixed new color on the palette
      and may still have a chance to
      direct the form
      stretch the canvas once again
for da Vinci
between a wheel and canvas
unfinished, musing
with Mona Lisa smile
turns to me

12/5/1986

Don't Take Pictures

I have no need of photographs
    frozen moments
    that fade in time and memory

I have instead
    soft, secret fingertips
    eyes deep, shimmering seas
    impish smiles
    warm laughter

    always here, always new

Don't take pictures, stop the magic
    let it live
    even as a dream

12/14/1986

This Pleasant Pain

What right have I to know this pleasant pain?
So often I have longed for such desire:
The promise in a touch as soft as rain
Yet burns my skin like drops of liquid fire;
Such visions of my life in dreamer's eyes
As haunt my nights and drive away all sleep;
Or nova smiles to brighten brightest skies
And pierce my heart with joys too late to keep.
The fleetest moments race against the past
Until my heart is beaten still with fears,
But I would want each aching hour to last
A day, a week, a month, a stretch of years.
Though I am sworn to live the life I do,
How can I cure my soul of wanting you?

12/14/1986

Bouquet

I'd give you flowers

    columbine for disloyalty?
    rue for sorrow?
    daisies for infidelity?
    or rosemary for remembrance?
    pansies for thoughts?
    fennel for flattery?
    violets for faithfulness?

No

I'd give you roses
    not yellow

    red

    scarlet with passion's heat
    plucked wild by the handful
    green and hurting with newness and life

    standing naked in the brambles
    both hands full
    dripping pain
    an offering

These flowers I'd give you.

1/6/1987

Chiaroscuro

Center the light
intense
focused
Surround it with shadows
growing into darkness and frame but drawn to the
light

of your smile

softened by visions in your
eyes
dreams of dreams and impossibilities
flowing out from the source yet always returning to
you.

4/13/1987

Michael D

Thanks
    for laughing at the same insanities 'til our eyes water
        hanging a puppet moose head in your pickup
        giving Clayton his first haircut
        being there (without being asked) when I'm away
        helping do the dishes after a two-family feast
        getting your own beer and bringing me one
        using the downstairs bathroom
        lending a hand, and anything else I need
        crying at a movie, "The Star-Spangled Banner," and
            sadness
        coming back from Nam
        talking about it
        listening to me talk
        understanding
        chewing out all four kids indiscriminately
        making sure I got home alright
        letting me know I'd been stupid
        celebrating my successes like they are your own
        appreciating our differences
        teaching me what you know
        growing happily older together
        discovering life with me
        being
my friend.

7/1/1987

The Romantic Reader's Valentine

"Love" grew from the pages of my books:

When very young
    I sought Rapunzel, hidden in her tower, to climb her golden
        braids,
    carried a glass slipper down my kingdom's midnight streets,
        and
    awoke from a poisoned sleep with first kiss of a snow white
        maiden;

As I grew older,
    valiantly I claimed Aleta, Queen of the Misty Isles,
    each afternoon in Lincoln green, rescued Marion from
        Prince John, and
    in trial by combat saved Rebecca, a lion-hearted, raven-
        haired Jewess;

Later still
    in fourteen lines I learned to count the ways I loved,
    and loving better after death found Juliet,
    lost the known world to an Egyptian serpent, and
    drowned a maid in flowers when she could not fathom my
        madness;

I thought I wanted comparisons,
>   but, like Petrarch's, my own Laura was unapproachable,
>   I searched in vain with Astrophel among the stars, and
>   although
>   I would not lie with false compare, did not want wiry hair
>   or reeky breath;

And I didn't really want trouble –
>   to drive Guinevere to fire or convent,
>   drink by mistake with Iseult the too strong potion,
>   or, choosing beauty, cause Helen's thousand ships to sail;

So now what?
>   Is Penelope still waiting for my odyssey to end?
>   Is Catherine keeping watch for me on the heights?
>   Does Aurora sleep on? Dreaming of our first dawn?

Must I wait an hundred years and find love yet only in the
>   pages of my books?

2/8/1988

The Love My Love Is Sending

(Variations on a Theme)

In each moment's briefest passing,
in each fleetest breath's light sigh,
is a lifetime's greatest blessing,
love to last until I die.

As the sun goes to its setting,
as the moon wanes in the night,
so, too, fades my regretting,
when I feel my love's delight.

With the cold of winter's graying,
with the coming of the storm,
I can hear my true love saying,
"Come, my love, I'll keep you warm."

'Though a story has an ending,
'though a song may not be sung,
yet the love my love is sending
keeps my heart forever young.

2/17/1988

Margaret's Waltz

Margaret, come with me. Dance the long night away
Here in my arms, where you know you belong.
Music will fill us. Our bodies will gently sway.
Heartbeat to heartbeat – no step can be wrong.

Feel, only feel, in the rhythms of loving me,
All of the music the world has to give.
Let it wash over you, lifting us on our sea,
Sailing and dancing the love that we live.

Oceans of music – a fanfare, a lullaby,
Whispering, swelling, until it's a storm.
Margaret, waltz with me. Dance the long night away
Here in my arms, your love's harbor from harm.

3/15/1988

Then Tears

The lines storm across the paper.
Now, too heavy to hold,
those few brief words drift away from trembling hands
and two once-joined lives shatter in the fall.
Then tears.

or

Suddenly
the dial tone is a monotonous dirge
accompanying the silent rending of a heart.
No warning.
Just the final, long distance soliloquy.
Then tears.

or

Cold, dead arms embrace, release.
Emptiness fills the new space.
Hands, hearts no longer touch.
Then tears.

Because I have already numbered each unwelcome drop,
catalogued every agonized stream,
perhaps there will be no need for them at

"Goodbye."

4/4/1988

Patience

If time melts, it does so with glacial slowness,
the minutes oozing across the landscape.
Even that marvel has its own vegetable speed –
greening or exploding or fading almost overnight,
yet moving across the earth in only centennial leaps.

And I sit with the patience of the tides,
chafing at the shore,
waiting for you
and the time that will race in breathless heartbeats
to my next waiting.

5/12/1988

Young Fire

It's in your eyes
new-kindled
ready

Don't fear it
flashing
timid

Fan the flame
encouraging
brash

Feed the light
confident
daring

Give it away
caring
loving

Teach it to others

6/9/1988

First Days of Summer Vacation

Close your searching eyes against the light
Rest your weary head against the sand
Feel the heat of day cool into night
Let the trials of life slip from your hand

Relax and dream your favorite dream
Sigh away the weighty cares

    Life is never what it seems!
    Changes come for one who dares!

But rest, be calm; for now, choose peace
Accept the summer sun's caress
Give your body and your mind well-earned release
You've worked so hard at doing more,
    Now work at doing less.

6/14/1988

Just One, Ours

We stood in the valley of an ancient sea,
a red rock Eden rising around us.
The ebb and flow of our emotions washed away
brief pasts and left us new to one another.

No tree rose between us and understanding
and so there was no pain, no banishment.
What we saw was an uncovered soul –
just one, ours – that one we share.

We share its passion and its tenderness
(for us and for our others).
We share its need and its giving
(for us and for our others).

We share ourselves with us and so many others
that there are times when we must fill ourselves
with us and with our others and so return
to look into our eyes again.

Stand and look into the sea
or drink the air from the shoulders of the world
or soar above the plains on red-tipped wings,
just feel again the touch of soul to soul.

We are more now than what we were
because we know the soul we share.
So much more remains for us to find within our selves,
the search will, thankfully, be a long one.

3/19/1990

Quiet Thunder

Comfortable and secure on my Iowa porch, I
enjoy distant flashes behind high, banked clouds and
strain to hear the quiet thunder of the storm.
The violence doesn't touch us here.

From any compass quarter the storms lose against the
                      unmoving middle.
But sometimes here
the earth itself becomes the wind and rises howling amidst
explosions of light. Then we burrow deep.

The next days, blinking away the brightness,
returning, we
shake our heads at the disturbance and sit back on
replicated porches to listen for the quiet thunder once again.

5/25/1990

Anima

With your eyes I see heaven in a rose.
You whisper to me in snowfall.
Music pulses in me with your rhythms.
Mountain sunshine flashes your smile.
    I breathe your sighs
        touch with your care
            hope with your innocence
                reach to your ambition.
Your spirit tempers me.
We are one soul
    inspiring double destiniess
cherishing at last our sharing.

12/1/1987

Animus

With your eyes I see Eden new made.
I hear your voice in thunder and in sunlight.
The earth's tide pulls me with your song.
Mountain sunshine flashes your smile.
    I breathe your calm
        touch with your tenderness
            hope with your exuberance
                reach with your daring.
Your spirit gives me wings.
We are one soul
    inspiring double destinies
cherishing at last our sharing.

3/22/1991

Other People's Children

Other people's children
    have my time:
        Before the sun I rise to seize the day for them
            to lead the way, to push to their discoveries,
            to explain what was and is and marvel
            at the new they see.

Other people's children
    have my hands:
        Throughout the day I hold the world for them
            to point to their lives' paths,
            to tend their hurts along the way, to button, paste,
            protect, applaud.

Other people's children
    have my heart:
        At end of day I stop to wonder at my care for them
            to weep in joy or sorrow at success or failure,
            (theirs or mine), to swell with pride
            at every goal attempted or dream first dreamed.

Other people's children
    have my life:
        Day in, day out, I give my life for them
            to make the world a better place,
            their lives predict and promise the future for us all.

Other people's children
    have the all of me:
        As every moment of my life
           I teach.

12/5/1991

Dance with Me

I remember

How we eyed one another like seventh graders across the floor
   of the Garden of the Gods

               Fear pounding in our hearts

Our first awkward steps, clinging to one another for support
   and new familiarity

             Need and longing clamoring alarms

Arm-in-arm on the sand, doe-si-doe, dodging the cold Pacific surf

             Joy, new joy, a fanfare in our eyes

Tango in the desert
   tap through the Underground
      soft shoe in the museum
         ballet in the rain of Puget Sound
           salsa in the night, in the night

             Heart strings taut and humming

We waltzed across the nation with our heads in the clouds

             "But we never danced… ."

3/1992

Heart to Hand

MAN: *(stage right)* Strength

WOMAN: *(stage left)* to Strength

    (face one another, right hand to right hand, clasped)

BOTH: We are yet opposed.

    (drop hands, then left hand to left hand, palm to palm)

WOMAN: Heart

MAN: to Heart

BOTH: We are yet alone.

    (drop hands, then Woman's right hand to
Man's left, palms together)

WOMAN: My Strength

MAN: Opens my Heart.

    (hands remain, then Woman's left hand to
Man's right, palms together)

WOMAN: My Heart

MAN: Is my greatest Strength.

    (hands remain)

BOTH: Together

    strong for one another,

Our Hearts

    open to All.

(Woman's right hand remains in Man's left,
turn to audience, outstretch outside arms).

7/30/1992

Dancing with Susan

No awkward first steps…
    you waltzed right up
    and swept me in.

No pas de deux…
    the floor is much too crowded!

Two-step and go,
    always on pointe to someone,
    something new.

But I'm never out of turn.
You tapped my trust
    and turn handsprings around me,
    relying on the constancy of love

and all that jazz.

12/4/1995

The Promise

(for S.B.)

An enthusiastic hand waves
expectantly
questing, demanding, hoping
pleading

       today

       tomorrow

Help

An encouraging heart smiles
knowingly
acknowledging, prodding, permitting
hoping

       today

       tomorrow

Help

4/13/2009

Sunshine

Sunrise
    flares of smiles
    ignite laughter
    illuminate dark hearts
    dry sad tears.
Days grow in sunshine
    bright moments stretch to years
    summer, fall, winter, spring…

Sunset
    is only Promise
    of a smiling, rising
Sun.

3/10/2010

Fixing Fence

(after "Mending Wall" by Robert Frost)

Something there is that doesn't love a fence,
those suburban property subdivisions of wood or
stone or wrought iron railing or un-naturally pristine PVC.
Each fall the faded trumpet vine that was so prolific on my
    west fence
must be trimmed and chopped and mulched.
By October it has begun to pull apart the dog-eared boards,
the summer's stalky branches, heavy leaves, and brassy
    trumpets
too much to bear.
I let my neighbor know beyond the fence,
and on a day we meet to prune the spindly vines and
    crumbling trunks.
We keep the fence between us.
To each the branches that have grown to each.
They seem to divide themselves evenly.
If one side is harvested before the other,
The fence it holds upright begins to lean.
We have no spell to make it balance.
This is no outdoor game. For men past middle age like us
The work is strenuous and tiring. It's work, and nothing more.
The vine has spread almost the length of our dividing fence.
"Most days I like this trumpet vine," my neighbor says.

He leaves unsaid that this day seems an exception.
I tell him that I'd rather it was just the fence.
He only smiles and I understand we'd miss the green and
    orange
and all the birds that roost in the summer cover.
When finished, we meet at the gates again and talk
of our families and work and what we'll do in spring again,
conversation started when first we met to trim the vine many
    years ago.
I remember then that "Good fences make good neighbors," but
    I think
it's just a trumpet vine.

11/15/2010

Grey Watcher

stealthy grey watcher
swift and sure on silent feet
glides through sun shadow

sound and scent ghost paths
friend and foe (feast and famine)
all mean survival

young and old follow
learn or lean on life and death
generations pass

pad on softly by
leave only footprints behind
vague grey memories

03/10/2011

Sarah Benck Serenade

Copper red halo
Glows in spotlight
Blues
Electrifying
Illuminating
Double-barreled
Angel voice
Fills hearts and halls
Roars whispers of
Love and loss
Heartache aftermath

4/10/2011

Cross Word Puzzle

shutupihateyou
youcannotdothat
itsmylifeyoucantmakeme
whydontyoulisten
whydontyouunderstand
idoidoyourenotlistening
whycantyouhearme
imtryingiloveyou

9/29/2011

Senioritis

(with apologies to Langston Hughes and Dr. Suess!)

What happens to a dream deferred,
and aspirations have been blurred?

Do goals dry up and cease to glow?
Are all aims missed, or don't you know?

Have you misplaced the why and how
of what is left
      or next
           or now?

When what you're doing now is a load,
and you feel yourself about to explode…

Your future's not a dream to lose.
Each step must be your best. You choose!

03/21/2012

Just to Be Clear: *The Pledge of Allegiance*

I	(me, myself alone, individually)
pledge	(promise, swear, avow)
allegiance	(loyalty, respect, service)
to	(toward, at, on)
the	(that one)
flag	(emblem, symbol, token, banner, standard, ensign)
of	(from, by, caused by)
the	(that one)
United	(joined, combined together, made one, in agreement and harmony)
States	(circumstances, attributes, conditions, position, rank, style, power, body, political organization)
of	(from, by, caused by)
America,	(The United States of America)
and	(in addition to)
to	(toward, at, on)
the	(that one)
republic	(representative government, democracy)
for	(in place of, in the interest of, in favor of, in honor of, in order to be)
which	(what one of several, the one that is meant)
it	(The United States of America)

stands,	(represents, symbolizes)
one	(single, unique)
nation	(stable community of people with a territory, history, culture in common)
under	(governed by, in the power of, obedient to, subordinate to, belonging to)
God,	(lord, deity, supreme being: e.g., Jehovah, Yahweh, Allah, Brahma, Buddha, Mazda, Ormazd)
indivisible,	(one nation of states united together to form one country, not separated into parts)
with	(along side of, near to, in addition to, in the company of)
liberty	(freedom, enfranchisement, power of choice)
and	(in addition to, also)
justice	(righteousness, fairness, rightfulness, truth, equity, constitutionality)
for	(in place of, in the interest of, in favor of, in honor of, in order to be)
all.	(every individual citizen and each united together)

10/6/2001-06/14/2012

Toss and Turn

Sleep comes
Dreams follow nothing
Good
I wake to
    Dreams
Nothing
good

11/03/2012

Dandelions &
Other Flowers

The first piece of my heart
was a bright lion's tooth
clutched in a toddling hand.

Then small purple baskets
were shards of young kisses
chased off on the first of May.

I danced around pieces
and petals of heartache
watered with crocodile tears.

Then truth and troth
walked a long aisle
strewn with the scent of forever,

But life's final season
is truly eternal
and the blossoms are all etched in stone.

From roots that run deep
come dreams of tomorrow –
no thorns or bare branches –

just flowers.

12/04/2013

Lonely

Lonely
is
    lost
in
red hair
green eyes
full lips
    your arms
Found
    Again.

12/16/2013

The Heart

The heart
opens to the warmth of need
  and needs the warmth;
reaches longingly to touch
  and longs for the reaching touch;
brightens to understanding
  and understands the brightness;
embraces openness
  and opens to an embrace;
    fills with love
      and fills
        with
          love.

12/23/2013

Charming Dreams

The Prince
 in castle-cold rooms of
-ever-after
 considers the eternity of
pursuit

> One hundred years asleep
> abruptly awakened in
> a dawn too bright

> Glass slipper dreams
> soon churlish forgeries
> kept in a pumpkin shell

> A panting beast
> who came with the bell
> traded for a rose

> Undone the braid
> the blindness passed
> the singer gone again

The dragons that guarded
each hopeful promise are
all dead

The separating sword
now sheathed
has turned to
rust

The roses so soon
withered and dead
rejected for
pricks
of thorns

He wonders what is left
but memory and fantasy
and years of longing and regret

Perhaps
he thinks
when it comes to that
he was better off
a frog

12/27/2013

Soliloquy

PART 1

I

PART 2

i

PART 3

I
stand apart
within the crowd
although i offer up
longing and love
sacrificial
me

01/03/14

Rainbow Bridge

Ride the grim horse, racing against ravaging time
    across the arcing radiance, hoping that somewhere
Over the outer limits on the other side, out beyond
    the only gate to otherwhere,
You understand that yesterday's yearning was simply
    yet again the question without an answer.
Gather together the grains of truth, sifted grams of
    fabled glory from Asgard to Ararat or wishful glimmers,
Bridging baleful brooding because your beloved is
    buried in the flower bed and you are left behind.
I insist in implying that within us lies infinity,
    inherent implications of immortality amid
Visions voiced in volumes of both vitriol and vainglory;
    Reach Out; Your Greatest Belief Is Victory.

01/13/2014

365 Days Later

Three chords into your favorite song
Our granddaughter smiles your smile
My fitted sheet is folded into a misshapen heap
Your name written inside an old album cover
White Christmas in July 15th movie listings
I dry the dishes I've washed by hand
First iris, sun on the deck, red-gold leaves, snowfall
Rendezvous Mountain and ski lifts
One of your earrings falls out of my suitcase
A hint of your perfume in an elevator
Old growth on the hydrangea needs trimming
Flashes of red in the snow is a cardinal at the feeder
Clouds open to sky the blue of your eyes
The waitress introduces herself with your name
I drive myself home
Fall asleep
Wake
Alone.
Tears don't come as often now

01/17/2014

About the Author

Daniel J. Cox is a retired college professor and high school English teacher living in Omaha, Nebraska. After 41 years teaching teachers and high school students in Iowa and Nebraska, he is spending his time catching up on his writing, his grandchildren, and Roots/Americana music in the thriving Omaha music scene. In addition to writing poetry since grade school, he is trying his hand at short essays, short fiction, and is working on his first novel. His short story, "Ambush," is forthcoming in *Fine Lines*.

Teachers and students are encouraged to contact Dan with questions or comments about the work in this volume. He has always explained that teaching is not what he does, but who he is, even in retirement!

Contact Dan at: drdancox01@gmail.com

8718504R00042

Made in the USA
San Bernardino, CA
19 February 2014